Let's Drive, Henry Ford!

by Peter and Connie Roop

SCHOLASTIC INC.

New York   Toronto   London   Auckland   Sydney
Mexico City   New Delhi   Hong Kong   Buenos Aires

For Father,
who enjoyed a drive
in the country

ISBN 0-439-67624-X

12 11 10 9 8 7 6 5 4 3 2 1   4 5 6 7 8 9/0

Printed in the U.S.A.   40
First printing, October 2004

Table of Contents

Introduction

Henry Ford is famous. He made many different kinds of cars. Do you know that Henry did not invent the car?

Henry was born on a farm in Michigan. Do you know that wolves could be heard in the woods when Henry was born?

Henry worked hard on the family farm. Do you know that Henry was determined to find a way not to do all of that hard work?

Henry loved to fix broken watches. Do you know that Henry repaired his neighbors' watches for free?

Henry loved to tinker with toys. Do you know why his brothers and sisters wouldn't let him play with their toys?

Henry was fascinated by the power of steam. Do you know that Henry made a steam whistle to scare his sister?

Henry liked to learn. Do you know that he never finished high school?

Henry left his family's farm to work with machines. Do you know he ran one of Thomas Edison's first electricity plants in Detroit?

Henry was fascinated with the idea of designing a horseless carriage. Did you know that other inventors succeeded before he did?

Henry dreamed of building a car to carry people. Do you know that he made millions of cars, trucks, and tractors?

Henry had many ideas. Do you know it was his idea to build cars quickly and inexpensively on an assembly line?

The answers to these questions lie in who Henry Ford was as a child and as a young man. This book is about Henry Ford before he made history.

1

Henry Ford Is Born

July 30, 1863, was another busy day on the Ford farm near Dearborn, Michigan. There were cows to milk. The horses needed water. The chickens had to be fed. The sheep were ready to be put into the pasture. There was wood to chop and hay to cut.

But before William Ford began his chores, he held Henry, his newborn son. Henry was the second child of William and Mary Ford. Henry Ford had been born at seven o'clock, just after sunrise. Before William went to work, he carefully put Henry in his wooden crib to sleep while Henry's mother rested.

Henry's father, William Ford, was twenty-one years old when he came to America with his family. The Fords were an Irish farming

family. They loved living on the land. But times were hard in Ireland. The potato crop had failed. People were starving. The Fords couldn't pay the rent on their land. They were forced to move.

Relatives in Michigan asked the Fords to join them in America. William sailed to America with his parents and his six younger brothers and sisters. Sadly, William's mother died on the journey. The Ford family landed in Quebec, Canada. They traveled west to Detroit, Michigan.

The Fords were glad to live in America. They owned their own fertile farm. They grew their own food. They built a log cabin and a shelter for their horses, cows, and oxen.

William worked on Patrick O'Hern's farm to make extra money. There he met Mary Litogot, the O'Herns' beautiful foster daughter. Mary's father had died in an accident. Mary's mother couldn't care for her family, so Mary lived with the O'Herns. The O'Herns loved Mary like a daughter.

William helped Mr. O'Hern build a two-story house with seven rooms. They built a picket fence around the house. William painted the house and fence bright white. The men also constructed a barn. Later, William purchased the house and farm from Mr. O'Hern.

William now had land and a house. He bought a horse-drawn buggy with a top, the first one in Dearborn. Now he was ready to marry.

On April 25, 1861, William Ford and Mary Litogot were married in Detroit. They celebrated their wedding with a dinner for friends and family in their new home.

The days were busy for William and Mary. William cared for the farm animals and his crops. He cut down trees and chopped wood. He made and repaired his own tools. He hunted and fished.

Mary cooked, washed, churned butter, made soap and candles, and gardened. She spun wool into yarn. She wove the yarn into cloth from which she made their clothes. She stitched quilts and knitted socks.

The Fords had a large garden. They grew cabbages, beets, turnips, carrots, and potatoes. William planted apple and pear trees. Mary canned the fruit. She stored the vegetables in the cool root cellar under the house.

By 1863, the year Henry was born, the Fords owned over two hundred acres of land. Even though they had neighbors, much of this part of Michigan was still wilderness. Huge trees towered toward the sky. Wolves howled. Deer, bears, and turkeys were plentiful.

Detroit was about ten miles away. Detroit was Michigan's biggest, busiest city. Forty-five thousand people lived in Detroit. Each year, thousands of other families passed through this city on their way west. Detroit was a good market for farmers like William and Mary Ford. One day, their son Henry Ford would make Detroit the worldwide center for the automobile industry. But that day lay far in the future for their baby boy.

2
Henry Grows Up

As soon as he could walk, Henry followed his father around the farm. He watched him work with his tools. Henry quickly learned what each tool was for and how to use it. He would have a lifelong love of tools and machines.

Before long, Henry had three brothers and two sisters: John, Margaret, Jane, William, and Robert. Henry's father built extra rooms onto the house. The children's room was upstairs. A long pipe from a downstairs stove heated their room.

As Henry grew up, his father taught him how to do many farm jobs. Henry learned to care for the farm animals. One of Henry's jobs was feeding the chickens. Henry didn't

like this job and said, "Chickens is fit only for hawks."

Henry also milked the cows. He didn't like this job, either. He said, "Milk is a mess." He knew milk was good for you, but it was just too much work to get it from the cows.

Henry learned how to plow straight rows, just like his father. He planted seeds. He chopped wood into kindling for his mother's stove. He carried water from the well.

Henry's father was patient, but he also was demanding. Once he showed Henry the correct way to do a chore, he expected Henry to do it that way every time. Henry liked living on the farm, but he didn't like all of the hard work. Sometimes Henry was tired of working by ten o'clock in the morning. He would go inside the house for a drink of water and never come back. Henry kept thinking that there must be easier ways to do things, ways that didn't require so much hard work.

One day, Henry decided to make the farm gates easier to open and close. The gates were heavy and hard to move. Each time Henry or his father came to the gates, they had to climb off their wagon, open the gates, drive the wagon through, then close the gates.

Henry decided to find a simpler way to open the gates. He made new hinges so the gates would be easier to move. He also made a device to open and close the gates so he wouldn't have to climb off the wagon to pass through.

Henry was fascinated with gears, wheels, sprockets, and chains. His pockets were full of screws, nails, pieces of string, nuts, springs, watch parts, and odd pieces of metal he found.

Henry's mother let him build a workbench in the dining room. This was Henry's private place. None of the other children were allowed to touch Henry's things.

One day, when Henry was seven, a farm-hand showed Henry how his watch worked. The man explained to Henry how the main-spring kept the wheels in motion and how the hands moved. From then on, Henry loved watches. Henry observed watchmakers work whenever he could.

Henry tinkered with broken watches on his workbench. One man said that clocks and watches "shuddered" when Henry came near. But Henry was patient and persistent. He solved the mysteries of how watches worked. He learned how to repair broken watches. He traded his marbles for watch wheels.

Henry made his own tools. He filed down nails to make screwdrivers. He made his own tweezers to pick up the tiny watch pieces. He made tools from knitting needles. Later in life Henry said, "My toys were all tools — they still are!"

Henry made toy sleighs and wagons. One winter, Henry saw some locomotives in Detroit. Locomotives are engines used to pull railroad cars. Henry decided to build his own train. After a snowfall, Henry took out his sled. He borrowed two kettles from his mother. He filled one kettle with hot coals, and he filled the other kettle with boiling water. Henry then stacked the two kettles. Steam from the hot water rose into the chilly air. Henry pulled his "locomotive" around the yard all day.

Henry's father had a workshop where he repaired farm equipment. Henry had his own workbench in the shop, too. Mr. Ford watched Henry's growing fascination with mechanical things. He didn't encourage Henry's interest in machines. He wanted Henry to be a farmer, not a mechanic.

Henry's mother, however, understood her son. She said that Henry was born a mechanic. Henry's sister Margaret said, "I think wheels were in his head."

Henry admired his mother. She worked hard to keep a good house and raise her family. When the children played outside and she worked inside, she watched them through the kitchen window. Henry's mother knew how to cheer up her children when they were sad. She knew how to comfort them when they were sick or hurt. She also knew how to encourage them.

3
Henry Learns Many Things

Henry learned many valuable lessons from his parents, especially his mother. He learned to work hard, be neat and clean, and always do his best. Henry always tried to live his life so his mother would be pleased by his decisions.

Henry's mother told him, "Life will give you many unpleasant tasks to do; your duty will be hard and disagreeable and painful to you at times, but you must do it." Henry believed these words all his life.

Henry's mother also taught him to always tell the truth. If Henry disobeyed his mother, she didn't raise her voice. Instead, she wouldn't speak to him or smile at him for a whole day. Henry said that when his mother did this, it "cut more deeply than a whip."

The most important lesson Henry's mother taught him was how to be happy with his family. She said, "If we couldn't be happy here in this house, we'd never be happy anywhere else."

Henry and his mother were so close that she could even guess what he was thinking. She would answer his questions before he even asked them.

Henry's mother also encouraged him. She let him have his workbench inside the house. She listened as he explained the mechanics of a machine. She was patient with his constant tinkering. Henry's brothers and sisters watched him tinker with things, too. But they didn't like it when he took their windup mechanical toys. They complained, "Don't let Henry have them! He just takes them apart."

Henry didn't play with their toys. He took them apart to find out how the toys worked. All his life, Henry Ford had to know how things worked.

Living on the farm, Henry learned to enjoy the natural world. One of his earliest memories was seeing a song sparrow's nest. His father showed Henry the four eggs in it. The nest was in a corner of the farmyard. Mr. Ford told Henry not to disturb it.

When the baby birds were born, Henry's father turned his plow away. He didn't want to hurt the baby birds. When Henry was an adult with his own farm, he told his workers not to bother any birds.

The Fords went to church on Sundays. Everyone piled into the buggy and bounced along the dirt roads. When the weather was too cold, Henry's mother shared Bible stories at home.

Sometimes, Henry and his brothers and sisters rode in the buggy to Detroit with their parents. When they couldn't go, Henry's mother brought candy home for them. Henry especially enjoyed red-and-white peppermint sticks.

Henry learned many things as he worked

on the farm and at his workbench. But his parents also wanted Henry to learn how to read, write, and do math.

On January 2, 1871, Henry was supposed to start school. But the snow was too deep to walk to school, so Henry's first school day was January 9. He was seven and a half years old.

Henry's mother packed his lunch in a pail. Henry walked two miles to the Scotch Settlement School. The redbrick school had only one room. It was built in 1861, two years before Henry was born.

Emily Nardin was Henry's first teacher. She taught grades one through eight. She rang the bell at nine o'clock. The students studied all day, with a half-hour recess in the morning and an hour for lunch. Miss Nardin sent her pupils home at four-thirty, before it got dark.

Between thirty and forty students went to Henry's school. Many older boys didn't come to school in the spring and fall. Instead, they

worked on their families' farms. The older boys came to school in the winter, when the fields didn't need work.

Henry could already read when he started school. So he read *McGuffey's Second Reader*. Children all over America read the popular *McGuffey's Readers* in school and at home. Stories in the *McGuffey's Readers* told students exactly how to behave. Bad boys would be punished. Good boys would become President.

Henry remembered one story all his life. It was about a boy who skipped school to go swimming. The boy drowned. Henry memorized the lines: "Do not stop to play on your way to school. Do not play with bad boys. They will lead you into harm."

The *McGuffey's Readers* also taught spelling, grammar, and speech. There were poems, patriotic stories, and words of wisdom. Henry memorized many stories and sayings. He often repeated them when he became famous.

4
Henry Experiments

Miss Nardin sat on a raised platform in front of the class. When someone got into trouble, he or she had to sit in front, right under the teacher's eye. Henry said, "You got a good view of the stove in that location." Henry must have gotten into trouble once in a while.

Edsel Ruddiman was Henry's best friend. They shared a double wooden desk. One day, Henry and Edsel carved their initials onto their desk. Their initials, H.F. and E.R., are still on the desk! This desk can be seen today in Greenfield Village in Dearborn, Michigan, a museum Henry created when he became famous.

Frank Ward was one of Henry's favorite

teachers. Henry said that Mr. Ward taught him how to think, "not with a lead pencil, but with my head." Mr. Ward said to Henry, "Henry, why don't you learn to do things in your head? Learn to count up numbers mentally." Henry later said, "That lesson has been of great value all through my life."

At home, Henry kept tinkering and learning, too. The Fords subscribed to many magazines and newspapers. They had a collection of their own *McGuffey's Readers* as well as a dictionary and a Bible for the children to read.

As much as Henry loved to learn, he also loved to play. He played jokes on his sisters and brothers. Henry's father was strict, but he enjoyed the jokes as long as no one was hurt.

Henry played jokes on his friends, too. But sometimes the jokes backfired. One day Henry switched his lunch sandwich for a friend's cake. Henry gobbled the cake, got sick, and was in trouble with his parents!

Henry and his friends swam in Roule Creek. Henry was the best swimmer. He dared to swim out farther than any of the other boys. Henry liked to fish and hunt, too.

In winter, Henry and his friends went ice-skating. Sometimes, when the ice was especially thick, they skated down Roule Creek to the Rouge River and into Detroit! Henry, who wanted to be the best at whatever he did, skated faster and farther than most of his friends. One day, Henry would build the world's largest automobile factory along the banks of the river where he skated as a boy.

Henry enjoyed "nutting parties" in the fall. He knew where the best walnuts, hickory nuts, and butternuts grew. Henry gathered nuts with his brothers and sisters. They enjoyed them throughout the winter.

In the spring, Henry helped tap maple trees. The Fords collected the sap, boiled it, and enjoyed the maple syrup. Henry liked to pour maple syrup over his popcorn!

Henry's days were very busy. Even when he went to school, he had to help on the farm. He split wood into kindling for his mother's stove. He had cows to milk, horses to har-

ness, and fields to plow, plant, and harvest. No matter how busy Henry was, however, he found time to tinker with his tools.

One day, when Henry was nine years old, he was riding a colt named Jennie. Suddenly, a cow stood up in a ditch. Jennie was frightened and galloped away. Henry fell off, but his foot was caught in the stirrup. Jennie dragged Henry all the way home! Henry could barely walk for days. After that, Henry added horses to the list of farm animals he didn't like.

On March 29, 1876, when Henry was twelve years old, his world changed. His loving mother died in childbirth. She was only thirty-seven years old.

Henry missed his mother. He missed her laughter and her patience with his experiments. Henry said, "The house is like a watch without a mainspring." Mainsprings made watches run.

Mr. Ford hired his twenty-year-old niece, Jane, to help with the children. He had a farm to run and a family to provide for.

Henry kept busy. He did his chores and

his schoolwork. He spent time at his work-bench. He went to local parties and outings with neighborhood friends.

Henry knew so much about watches that he fixed his neighbors' watches for fun. He didn't charge them, because Henry liked the challenge of figuring out what was wrong with each watch and repairing it.

One hot July day after his mother had died, Henry was riding with his father to Detroit. Their horse plodded along, pulling their wagon over the rough road. Suddenly, Henry heard a loud noise ahead of them. He stared in amazement at a steam-powered machine chugging their way!

This was the first machine Henry had ever seen that moved on a road without horses pulling it. This huffing, puffing, roaring machine moved under its own power!

Later in his life, Henry said, "I can remember that engine as though I had seen it only yesterday. I was off the wagon and talking to the engineer before my father knew what I was up to."

5
Henry Experiments
with Steam

A man named Mr. Reden drove the rattling machine. Smoke poured out of its smokestack. Steam hissed from its fat, round boiler.

Mr. Reden proudly showed Henry how the machine worked. He told Henry that the motor spun around two hundred times a minute! Mr. Reden could harness his engine to a saw to cut boards. He could also use it to pull stubborn stumps out of the ground.

Henry never forgot the thrill of seeing his first steam-powered road machine. Later, Henry said that on that day, he began dreaming of creating his own machine to help farmers. He also began thinking about a machine that would carry people.

In 1876, the United States was one hundred years old. There were celebrations all over America. The biggest celebration, the Centennial Exhibition, was in Philadelphia, Pennsylvania.

Henry's father read about the Centennial Exhibition. He talked about the wonderful machines that would be on display. There would be steam engines that pulled heavy loads. There were steam plows that could do the work of many horses. There were dozens of other special mechanical exhibits. Thomas Edison would have a display there.

Mr. Ford talked about these modern marvels with his neighbors. He talked about them with Henry. Henry read about them, too. He dreamed of seeing these wonderful new machines in action. Henry was especially interested in the machines that would make life easier for farmers.

Mr. Ford decided to go to Philadelphia that fall, but Henry was too young to go with him. When Henry's father returned, he shared what he had seen with Henry. He told Henry about Independence Hall, where the Declaration of Independence had been signed. He also told him about seeing the hand and torch of the Statue of Liberty, which were on display.

Henry listened politely and patiently, but he really wanted to hear about machines. Finally, Mr. Ford told him about a steam engine that was two stories tall, the biggest engine in the world! He told Henry about powerful locomotives that were being built to move heavier loads. He told Henry about many new machines to make farmers' lives easier.

Henry's father brought him catalogs showing the machines. Henry studied these pictures for hours. He thought about steam power day and night. He began experimenting in the kitchen. He would put a teakettle on the hot stove and watch the steam hiss out.

One day, Henry decided to play a joke on his sister Margaret. Henry made a little brass tube and filled it with water. He made a small valve to fit on the top. He took a tiny watch wheel and attached it to a hole in the valve.

When Margaret wasn't looking, Henry put his invention on the hot stove. The water boiled and made steam. The steam rushed out with a shrill whistle that made Margaret jump. Henry laughed each time he scared his sister.

Later, when Henry was a steam-machine expert, Margaret returned the steam-whistle toy to Henry. Henry treasured it all his life because it reminded him of his first steam experiments.

Henry made what he called a steam "puffer." He took an old dishpan and an oilcan and made his own steam machine. He partly filled the oilcan with water. He started a fire in the dishpan to heat the water. Then Henry put four small fans on a rod above the hole in the oilcan's top. The wood burned, the water boiled, and steam jetted out of the hole and turned the fans.

Henry was proud of his "puffer." He took it to school to show his friends. The boys set up the "puffer" near a fence. They started the fire in the dishpan. Unfortunately, the fence caught on fire, too!

Henry's father rebuilt the fence. Henry and his friends were punished. Henry's teacher said no more steam experiments at school!

Once, one of Henry's steam experiments blew up. Henry's lip was cut. He had a scar the rest of his life. His friend Robert Blake was hit in the stomach with a piece of flying metal and was knocked out! Henry knew he had to be much more careful with his experiments.

6
Henry Leaves the Farm

Henry did another experiment that caused trouble. During recess, Henry and his friends built a dam on a small creek near the school. They collected stones and placed them in the creek. Slowly, their dam grew taller and taller. Finally, the dam was finished. A small lake of water backed up behind the dam.

A powerful stream of water flowed over in one place, just as they had planned. Henry put a paddle wheel into the stream of water. The water made the wheel spin faster and faster.

The boys enjoyed watching their water-wheel spinning. Then the teacher rang the bell. Henry and his friends ran back into school. By the time school got out, they had forgotten about their spinning waterwheel.

All night long, water backed up behind their dam. It flooded a farmer's field. The next morning, the farmer found his field under water! He made the boys remove the dam.

One day, Henry learned that the railroad bridge over Roule Creek was going to be repaired. Henry rushed down to see the machines at work. There was a train engine and three flatcars with cranes. The cranes lifted out old pieces of the bridge and put in new pieces.

A message came that two trains from Detroit needed to cross the bridge. Work stopped. The work train began chugging toward Dearborn in order to clear the tracks.

When the train engineer looked down, he saw Henry sitting on the cowcatcher on the front of the engine! The cowcatcher is a metal guard in front of a locomotive. It is there to "catch" cows wandering on the tracks and to push them out of the way. Henry called to his friends to join him. But the engineer ordered Henry to get off the cowcatcher and stay off. When the engineer wasn't looking, however, Henry and his friends jumped onto the flatcars and rode into Dearborn.

Henry also had a special workbench in his bedroom. He did experiments at his workbench late at night. A lamp on the table gave him light, and a lantern on the floor kept his feet warm. If his father came to see what Henry was doing up so late, Henry could fold the workbench and slide it under his bed.

Henry often went to Detroit with his father. They took hay, grain, and wood to sell. They also sold apples, potatoes, and other farm products. Henry sometimes rode on top of a load of hay or bounced along in the buggy. In the winter, Henry rode in a bobsled loaded with firewood.

Henry got to know his father's customers and friends in Detroit. James Flowers owned a machine shop. He was a friend of the Fords. Henry enjoyed visiting Mr. Flowers's shop. Henry stared at the many machines for cutting steel, shaping copper, and making metal parts. Mr. Ford knew Henry was fascinated by machines, but he still wanted Henry to become a farmer.

One morning in 1879, the Ford children prepared to go to school. Henry left with the others, but he didn't go to school. Instead, he walked to Detroit! He had made up his mind that his school days were finished. He wanted to work with machines and not on a farm. Henry was sixteen years old. He felt he could make up his own mind about his future.

Henry stayed with his aunt, Rebecca Flaherty, his father's sister. He began working as an apprentice in Mr. Flowers's machine shop.

Mr. Flowers and his men made things out of brass and iron. They made water valves and valves for steam engines, fire hydrants, and steam whistles. Henry earned two dollars and fifty cents per week while he learned the jobs. He worked sixty hours each week! Mr. Flowers was pleased to have Henry, especially because Henry knew so much about machines and was so skilled with his hands.

To make extra money, Henry repaired

watches at Magill's Jewelry Shop. Henry repaired watches in a back room. Mr. Magill was afraid that if his customers saw such a young man working on watches, they would think Henry couldn't do a good job!

Henry was paid fifty cents a night for six hours of work. Henry Ford didn't like hard, heavy farmwork, but he didn't mind working hard with watches and machines.

Henry came home on weekends to share his adventures, help his father, and repair his neighbors' farm machines. In his spare time, Henry studied engines and read about them. Henry experimented with engines in his shop. He was happiest working with steam engines.

Later, Henry left Mr. Flowers's shop and worked as an apprentice for the Detroit Dry Dock Company, a larger machine shop. At Dry Dock, Henry learned about more than just machines. One day, Henry struggled to push a heavy wheelbarrow up a ramp. Frank Kirby, an engineer, said to Henry, "Stick in your toenails, boy, and you'll make it!" Henry said, "I've been sticking in my toenails ever since."

7

Henry Works and Dreams

Henry worked so hard at the Detroit Dry Dock Company that he finished his apprenticeship in less than three years.

One of Henry's first jobs was making streetcars, but he got fired after six days. When a machine broke down, none of the older workers could fix it. Henry immediately saw what was wrong and repaired the machine. Instead of a reward for his efforts, Henry was fired for knowing too much! Henry wrote later, "I learned then not to tell all you know."

That summer, Henry was living at the Ford farm. He heard that his neighbor Jim Gleason's Westinghouse steam engine had broken down. Henry asked if he could fix the engine. He wasn't sure if he could fix it, but he was determined to try. Henry said, "I was unwilling to be beaten by an engine."

Henry went to work. Before long, he understood what was wrong. He said, "Getting a grip on the engine, I got a grip on myself."

Henry did such a good job that Mr. Gleason hired him to work his engine. Henry was paid three dollars a day. Henry went from farm to farm cutting clover, hauling heavy loads, cutting cornstalks, grinding feed, and sawing wood with the steam engine.

Henry knew so much about the Westinghouse steam engine that he got a job working for the Westinghouse Company. He traveled around Michigan setting up and repairing the big, heavy farm engines.

Henry knew that these machines were too large and too expensive for most farmers. Henry realized that farmers needed a lighter kind of tractor that didn't cost much. Henry kept this idea in mind for many years.

Henry planned to go into the watchmaking business. He would build a factory and make two thousand watches a day. He would

sell each watch for thirty cents. Then Henry sat down and did the math to see how much money he would make. He calculated he would need to make and sell six hundred thousand watches a year. Henry knew he could never sell that many watches. But Henry knew he wanted to make something that people needed, to build it well, and to sell it cheaply. Henry wondered what that product could be.

Henry remembered the day when he was twelve years old and had climbed aboard a steam machine rolling down the road. He wondered if he could build a machine that didn't need horses to move it from place to place. Henry knew his machine would have to be light. It would need some kind of fuel to power it. Steam engines were powerful, but they needed lots of wood or coal to keep them going.

Henry thought maybe electricity or gasoline might solve the fuel problem. He began to learn all he could about these fuels.

In 1884, Henry returned to the Ford farm to work and think. Henry's father hadn't given up on Henry becoming a farmer. Mr. Ford gave Henry an eighty-acre farm only one mile away from the Ford farm. The soil was good and there was lots of wood.

Henry set up a steam sawmill. He cut his own logs into lumber to sell. His neighbors brought their logs to Henry to cut, too. Henry cut boards. He built his own house.

While Henry was working, he was dreaming, reading, and planning. Henry read everything he could about the new gasoline engines.

One day Henry went to church with his sister Margaret. The sermon was called "Hitch Your Wagon to a Star."

On the way home in their horse-drawn buggy, Henry told Margaret, "That's what I am going to do." His "star" would be a horseless buggy to carry people.

8

Henry Moves to Detroit

In the summer of 1887, Henry met Clara Bryant at a dance. He enjoyed dancing with her. Henry showed Clara a watch he had made. Clara was impressed by Henry. She called him a "very sensible and serious-minded young man."

In the fall of 1887, Henry proved his skill with machines. His father had land that was covered with tree stumps. Mr. Ford was going to use his oxen to pull out the stumps.

Henry had an idea! He borrowed Mr. Gleason's steam engine. Henry quickly and easily pulled out the stumps. Even Mr. Ford was impressed by his son's work. Henry began giving Clara rides on the steam machine. He told her about his dream to make life easier for farmers. Clara listened to Henry. She wanted to be part of his dreams, too.

On April 11, 1888, Henry and Clara were married. This was also Clara's birthday! The newlyweds moved into the old farmhouse on Henry's farm.

Henry worked hard on his farm. He cut more boards and built a new house for Clara. But he couldn't forget all of the machines he had seen in Detroit. And he couldn't forget his idea of a horseless carriage.

Clara wondered how Henry could build such a machine. Clara was confident that Henry could make anything he set his mind to, even a horseless carriage. She just didn't know where Henry would find the time and money to build it.

After three years of living on the farm, Henry was ready for something different. He had money in the bank. He wanted to learn more about the electricity that was beginning to light Detroit homes and businesses. Henry got a job with the Edison Illuminating Company in Detroit.

It nearly broke Clara's heart to leave their farm and home. But she understood that Henry would be unhappy if they stayed. In 1891, the Fords loaded their furniture onto a hay wagon and moved to Detroit.

Henry's hours were from six o'clock at night until six in the morning. He was paid forty dollars a month. Henry walked home early in the morning thinking about his horseless carriage.

One day at work, a steam engine broke down. No one knew how to fix it, except Henry. He rolled up his sleeves and went to work. Before long, the engine was running again. Henry got a raise of five dollars a month for his quick work!

Henry and Clara moved to a bigger, better home on Bagley Avenue. Henry set up his workbench in a brick shed in the backyard. He bought a bicycle and a camera. And he began buying and making parts for his horseless carriage.

Henry had his own ideas for the horseless carriage. He realized that electricity in batteries wouldn't work for his horseless carriage. They were too heavy and they quickly ran out of power. He decided a gasoline engine would be best.

Other inventors, however, had the same ideas. A magazine called *The Horseless Age* wrote that, in 1892, three hundred men were working on horseless carriages.

Clara worried about their shrinking bank account. But her hands were full running their home and caring for their baby boy, Edsel. Edsel had been born on November 6, 1893. The doctor had come on his bike! Later, Henry always repaired the doctor's car for free.

Henry's work at the Edison Illuminating Company was so good that he was promoted. His salary jumped to ninety dollars a month.

In December of 1893, Henry decided it was time to build his first gasoline engine. He collected, bought, and made the parts he needed. He talked with fellow engineers about the best way to build the engine. He sketched his plans and built his engine.

On Christmas Eve, Henry decided to test his engine. He needed electricity to spark the gasoline so it would burn and power his engine. Henry had no electricity in his shop, so he carried his engine into the kitchen. Henry clamped the engine to a board by the sink. He connected a wire to the electric light.

Clara wasn't too happy about this invasion of her kitchen, especially on Christmas Eve. But she believed in Henry and helped him.

Henry handed her an oilcan filled with gasoline. Clara's job was to drip gasoline into the engine while Henry gave it electricity.

Suddenly, the lights dimmed. The engine roared to life! Henry ran the engine for thirty seconds. His test engine worked.

Now Henry had to build an engine big enough to power a horseless carriage! He turned all of his extra energy to solving the problem of building a machine to carry people. He was now chief engineer at Edison and worked long hours. But he still found time to think, read, and experiment. People wondered when Henry ever slept!

9
Henry's Horseless Carriage

Henry learned that other inventors had already succeeded in making horseless carriages. In Paris, they were used as wagons, carriages, and ambulances. In England, a prince owned a horseless carriage.

But Henry Ford wasn't worried. He knew that one day he would succeed. His goal was to make his vehicle work, then make it cheaper and better so more people could buy it.

Henry wasn't just building a heavy wagon with an engine. His machine would be light, rugged, fast, and reliable.

Henry kept designing, building, experimenting, and tinkering. He built a gas motor. He built a frame. He added a bicycle seat to sit on. He put on bicycle tires. He had a handle for steering. But Henry had no brakes. He would stop the carriage by turning off his engine. Henry called his invention a quadricycle because it had four wheels. "Quad" means four.

On June 4, 1896, Henry was ready to try his quadricycle. He was ready to test his machine. Clara came to watch. Henry realized he had made a big mistake! His machine was too large to fit through the shed doors. As usual, Henry Ford quickly solved the problem. He took an axe and knocked out bricks until the shed door was big enough to fit through.

Henry climbed onto his machine. He started the engine and it roared to life. Henry's friend Jim Bishop climbed onto his bike. Jim would ride ahead to keep people out of Henry's way.

Henry gave his motor more gas. Slowly, the quadricycle rolled out of the shed. Henry steered down the alley and turned onto Bagley Avenue. Jim pedaled ahead. Clara watched

as Henry turned a corner and rode into history. Henry didn't go very far. A nut fell off, and Henry's machine sputtered to a stop. Henry and Jim pushed it to the Edison Illuminating Company, where Henry got a new nut.

A small audience gathered to watch Henry drive his horseless carriage home. He proudly parked it in the shed. Henry Ford had successfully made his first car!

The next day, Henry installed a buggy seat so he could take Clara and their son Edsel for a ride. The Ford family amazed people as they chugged past in Henry's horseless carriage. The carriage made the sound *chucka-chucka-chucka-chucka-chuck*. They had never seen anything like it on the streets of Detroit!

Henry decided to test his car by driving to Dearborn to see his relatives. Once again, Jim Bishop rode ahead on his bike to warn folks that Henry was coming. The roaring engine frightened horses as Henry's car bumped along the rough road.

Henry's father was interested in Henry's car, but he refused to ride in it. He was proud of Henry and what he had invented. Mr. Ford, however, still believed Henry should be a farmer. He thought Henry's car was just another one of Henry's toys.

Henry knew better. He knew that if he could build one automobile, he could build more. He knew people were very interested in his horseless carriage. When Henry drove it in Detroit, people stopped and stared. They were so curious about Henry's car that he had to chain it to a lamppost when he wasn't in it. If he left his car alone, someone usually tried to drive it!

Henry got into trouble with the police. His car was causing traffic problems. It frightened horses, and they would stop pulling their wagons and buggies. This created traffic jams.

Henry finally asked the mayor for a special permit to drive his car in Detroit. Henry Ford was the first person to get a driver's license!

10
Henry Makes History

Henry was ready to build a better automobile. After he drove about one thousand miles, he sold his first car for two hundred dollars. That was the first Ford car ever sold!

Henry took the money and built another car. The second car was like the first car, but lighter.

For the next few years, Henry kept experimenting to make a better engine. He still worked for the Edison Illuminating Company. In 1899, Henry was offered a top job with the company, but only if he gave up working on his gas engine.

Henry had confidence in himself. Clara had confidence in Henry. Instead of taking the job,

Henry quit! Now he would work full-time in the automobile business.

Henry had friends who joined him in forming a company to make cars. Henry knew about machines, but he had much to learn about running a company to sell cars. For three years, Henry made cars but sold very few. Most people thought the car was just an expensive toy. Henry believed just the opposite.

After three years, Henry quit his business. He continued to experiment with making his car cheaper and faster. He learned how to operate a business better by himself. Henry was determined to once again have his own car company where he would be the boss.

Henry wanted people to know about his automobile, so he began to enter car races. He won the first race he was ever in against the best racer in America! Henry built two race cars. One was the "Arrow." The other was the "999." The cars were big, noisy, and fast. Henry said going over Niagara Falls would have been easier than riding in one!

Henry wanted to race the "999" in a big race, but the car was too hard for him to handle alone. Henry asked Barney Oldfield, a bicycle racer, if he would be willing to drive the "999." Barney was willing to drive anything on wheels. Barney learned to drive the racer in a week.

Barney climbed behind the wheel. He said, "Well, this chariot may kill me." Henry cranked the engine. It roared, and the race began. Barney drove Henry's car as fast as he could. He won the race by half a mile!

Henry built a fast car and he let people know about it. Winning the race gave Henry Ford and his automobiles lots of free publicity.

A week later, Henry started the Ford Motor Company. He built a car he called the "Model A." Henry sold 1,708 Model A cars in his first year. He realized that in order to sell more cars, he had to build them faster and more cheaply.

Henry thought about a solution. He knew his workers had to walk back and forth to get pieces to add to each car. Henry had an idea.

Why not bring the pieces to the worker? Even better, why not have each worker stay in one place and do one job? A piece would come to him, he would add the piece, and the car would move to the next worker. This would save time and money. Henry could "assemble" cars faster and cheaper on his assembly line.

Henry worked hard to improve his cars. He improved the motors. He made them lighter. He wanted them to be well built. Henry believed that if one of his cars broke down, it was his fault!

Henry Ford also made cars less expensive. He dreamed of making a car that anyone could afford.

Henry Ford's biggest success was his Model T car. The first Model T's were built in 1908 when the Ford Motor company was five years old. The Ford company sold 10,607 cars! A Model T sold for about $850.

The Model T was a simple car to build, own, and drive. Henry kept costs down. One simple idea was that all Model T's were the

same color. Henry said, "Any customer can have a car painted any color that he wants so long as it is black."

Henry Ford went on to build many more types of cars. His creation of an inexpensive "horseless carriage" helped millions of people. People could travel to places they had never been before. They could visit friends and family. Products could be shipped in trucks.

Henry also worked long hours to make another of his dreams come true. Under his guidance, Ford factories made Ford tractors. These tractors made farm life much easier. Who could have known that Henry Ford, born that hot July morning in 1863 on a small Michigan farm, would change the world?